HISTORY OPENS WINDOWS

The Ancient Egyptians

JANE SHUTER

Heinemann Interactive Library
Chicago, Illinois

© 1998 Reed Educational & Professional Publishing
Published by Heinemann Interactive Library,
an imprint of Reed Educational & Professional Publishing,
Chicago, IL
Customer Service 888-454-2279

Printed in Hong Kong, China

04 03 02 01 00
10 9 8 7 6 5 4

The Library of Congress has cataloged
the hardcover version of this book as
follows:
**Library of Congress Cataloging-
in-Publication Data**
Shuter, Jane.
　　The ancient Egyptians / Jane Shuter.
　　　p.　　cm. -- (History opens windows)
　　Includes index.
　　Summary: Describes life in ancient
Egypt, including farming, religion,
government, and medicine.
　　ISBN 0-431-05705-2 (lib. bdg.)
　　1. Egypt--Civilization--To 332 B.C.--
Juvenile literature.　　[1. Egypt--
Civilization--To 332 B.C.]　　I. Title.
II. Series.
DT61.S65　　　　1997
932--DC21　　　　　　　　96-53256
　　　　　　　　　　　　　　　　AC

Paperback ISBN 1-57572-590-8

Acknowledgments
The author and publishers are grateful to the
following for permission to reproduce copyright
photographs:
British Museum, pp. 7, 8, 12, 16/17, 19, 22,
25, 27, 29 (top), 31; Robert Harding Picture
Library, p. 2; Michael Holford, p. 21; Wellcome
Institute Library, p. 28; Hulton Picture Company,
p. 29 (bottom).

Cover photo © Werner Forman Archive/British
Museum, London

Contents

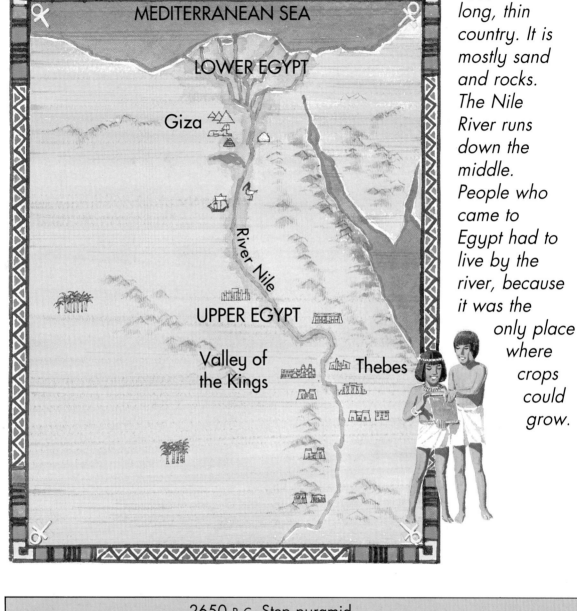

MEDITERRANEAN SEA

LOWER EGYPT

Giza

River Nile

UPPER EGYPT

Valley of
the Kings

Thebes

Egypt is a long, thin country. It is mostly sand and rocks. The Nile River runs down the middle. People who came to Egypt had to live by the river, because it was the only place where crops could grow.

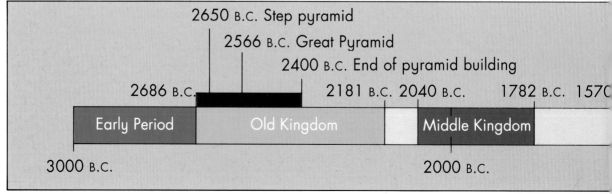

2650 B.C. Step pyramid
2566 B.C. Great Pyramid
2400 B.C. End of pyramid building

| 2686 B.C. | | 2181 B.C. | 2040 B.C. | 1782 B.C. | 157C |

| Early Period | Old Kingdom | | Middle Kingdom | |

3000 B.C.   2000 B.C.

At first, the Egyptians lived in small groups. Later they formed two large groups. One group lived in Upper Egypt, and the other lived in Lower Egypt.

We say that Ancient Egyptian civilization began when these two groups joined. This civilization lasted a long time. It started in about 3000 B.C., when the people of Upper and Lower Egypt started to work together. It ended in 30 B.C., when the Romans took over. Sometimes there were wars, which caused confusion and starvation. The times of peace were called the Early Period, the Old Kingdom, the Middle Kingdom, the New Kingdom, and the Late Period. These are marked on the time line below.

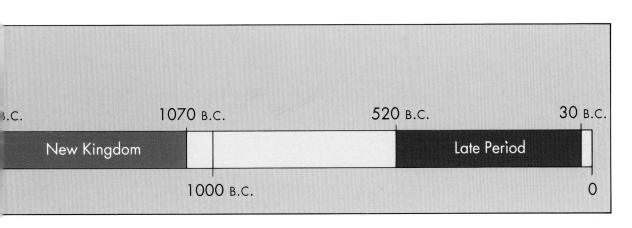

The Nile River

The Nile River floods every year. As the water goes down, it leaves behind rich soil. The land that has been flooded is the only place where crops can grow.

People lived by the river because they could grow things there. The Egyptians wanted to grow more crops. But to do this they had to control the water. They had to stop some of the flood water draining back into the river. They also had to find a way to get water from the river all year round.

The Ancient Egyptians invented the shadoof, shown here, to lift water from the Nile River. They are still used today.

The Egyptians got more than water from the Nile. Here we see a nobleman hunting river birds to eat. The people also ate fish and used reeds to make baskets and boats.

The Egyptians saw that the flood water could be held back with ponds and canals. Then they could use the water. It was hard work to make the ponds and canals. The Egyptians had to clear and repair them all the time. They could only do this if they all worked together.

Farming

The Egyptians farmed the land when the flood waters of the Nile River went down. They had to grow crops that would be cut before the next flood. The most important crops were wheat and barley, which were used to make bread and beer. These were what most Egyptians ate and drank.

Another important crop was flax, used to make cloth. The Egyptians grew fruit and vegetables, too. They ate a lot of onions and garlic, dates, and grapes.

The Egyptians grew grapes to eat and to make wine.

Farmers used animals to help plant the seeds.

The Egyptians kept geese and cows to eat. They also hunted river birds and fish. The Egyptians had no farm machines, so they used animals for some jobs. Goats and sheep pressed the seed into the ground with their feet as soon as it was planted. An ox pulled the plow, and trampled the grain to get the husks off.

The pharaoh

The Egyptians had to work together to control and farm the Nile River. People work together better if there is someone in charge. This person can make sure that all the work is done at the right time. In Egypt this person was called the pharaoh. He was seen as more like a god than just a person.

The Egyptians always had a pharaoh, unless they were fighting each other. When they fought, there was no one to run the country, so people were fighting, not farming. Many died in the fighting. Those who were not killed were likely to starve, because there was not enough food.

Pharaoh Tutankhamun's sarcophagus shows him holding signs for Upper and Lower Egypt. He has the goddesses of both parts on his crown. This is to show that he rules all of Egypt. You can find out more about a sarcophagus on page 19. Tutankhamun can also be spelled Tutankhamen.

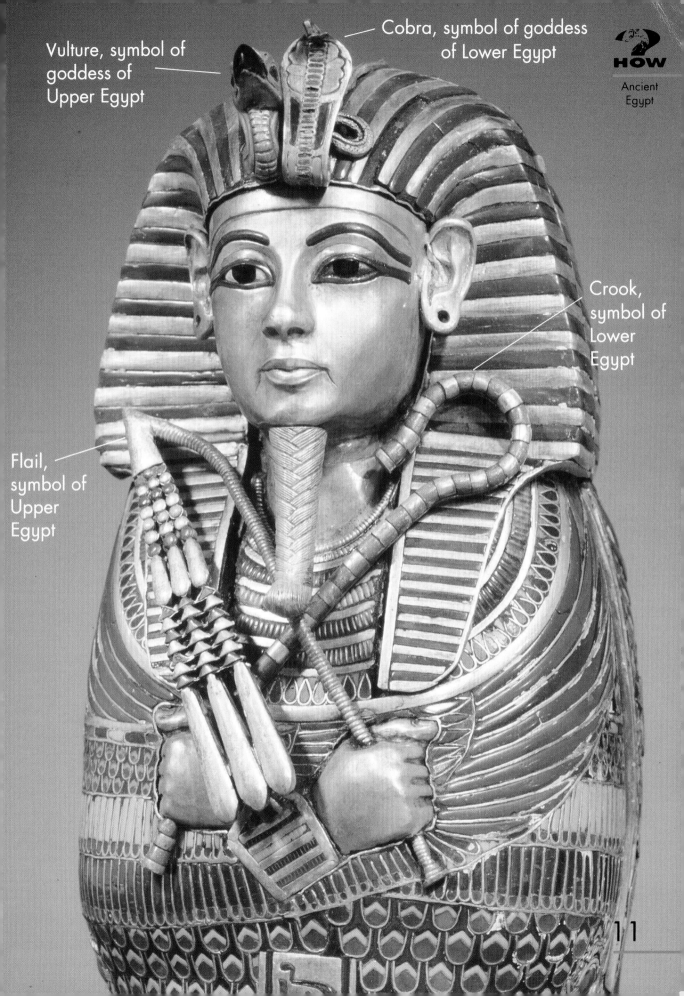

Vulture, symbol of goddess of Upper Egypt

Cobra, symbol of goddess of Lower Egypt

Crook, symbol of Lower Egypt

Flail, symbol of Upper Egypt

11

How Egypt was ruled

The scribes were the only people who could write. This skill made them important, because they could check all the food that was stored. Here a scribe is counting the geese.

On the next page is a picture that shows how the Egyptians divided up the work. The pharaoh was at the top, giving out the work. Under him were the viziers, high priests, and nobles. The Egyptians thought that all jobs were important except for those of the slaves, which were at the bottom. The Egyptians thought that their jobs were not very important.

Pharaoh Queen

Nobles Grand Viziers of Upper and Lower Egypt High Priest and
High Priestess

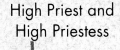

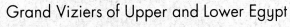

Governors

Craftsmen Artists Scribes Tax Gatherers Priests Priestesses

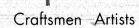

Builders Farmers Scribes Wab

Slaves

Trade

The Egyptians did different jobs. Some were farmers, and others were fishermen. Some made shoes, while some brewed beer and made bread. They did not have money to buy these things from each other. Instead, they traded with each other to get the things that they wanted.

Markets were often located by the river. They were where most trading was done.

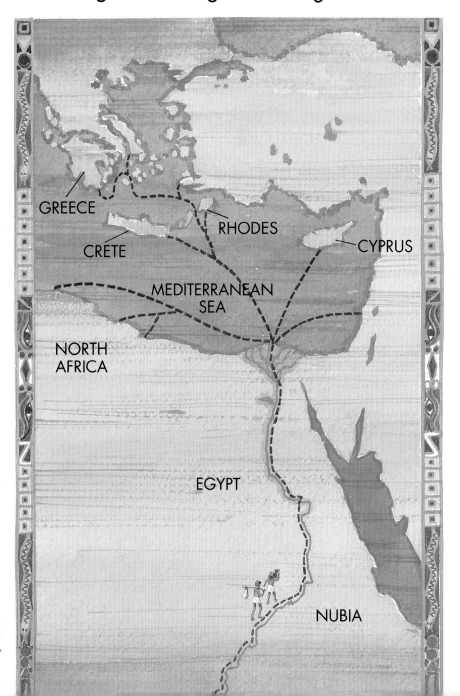

GREECE

CRETE

RHODES

CYPRUS

MEDITERRANEAN SEA

NORTH AFRICA

EGYPT

NUBIA

This map shows places with which the Egyptians traded.

The Egyptians also traded with other countries. They made more rope and flax than they needed. They often had more wheat than they would need in the coming year. They traded their extra supplies for things that they did not have, like wood, olive oil, silver and gold. They traded with other countries in the Mediterranean, mostly by boat.

Gods and goddesses

The Egyptians had lots of gods. Some of the gods were known by everyone. Other gods were only known by people in a certain area. The Egyptians saw important things, like the sun or the Nile River, as gods. They often drew gods with animal heads.

Egyptians prayed to different gods at different times. If they thought that the Nile River was not going to flood, they prayed to the river goddess, Hapi. If a child was ill, they prayed to Bes, god of children, or Imhotep, god of medicine.

The Egyptians saw gods all around them, all the time. They wanted to pray often, so each house had a shrine. This was a place to pray at any time. They built big temples, which they used on special days.

The gods judge a dead man. They balance his heart against the feather of truth. If he has been good, he can go to the Fields of Iaru (Heaven). If he has been bad, Ammut eats him.

Mummies

The Egyptians thought that people who died went to a new world. Because the people would need their bodies in the new world, their bodies had to be kept from going bad.

To make a mummy, the Egyptians first removed the soft insides. They hooked the brain out through the nose. They rubbed oils on the body. Then they wrapped layers of cloth around it.

These Egyptian priests are oiling and wrapping a body.

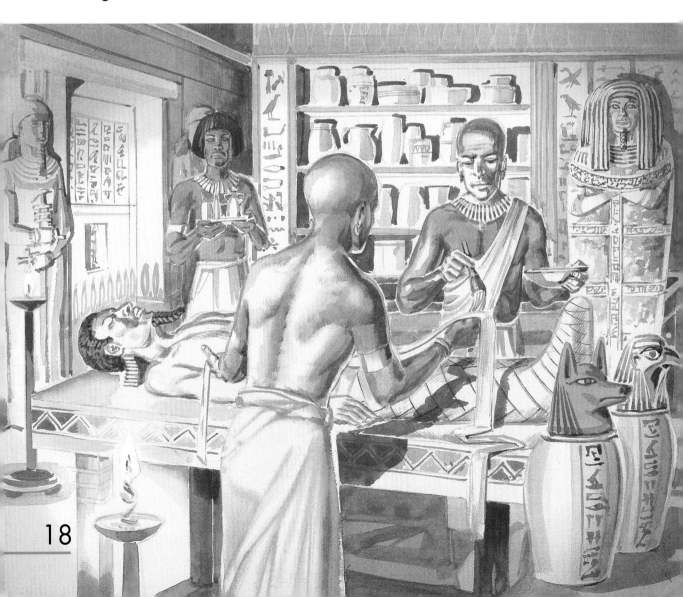

18

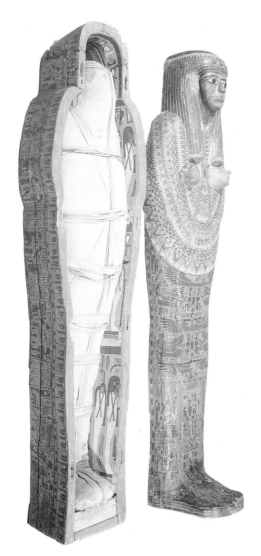

*A priestess
in her
sarcophagus,
which shows
what she
looked like.*

They sometimes gave the mummy a face
mask. It looked like the person did in real
life. A rich person would have their jewels
put on it. The mummy was put in a painted
case called a sarcophagus. The mummies
were buried in the ground or put in tombs.
Only some of the first pharaohs had
pyramids. Most of them were buried in
tombs cut in the rock in the Valley of Kings.

Pyramids

Only the pharaohs were buried in pyramids. Pyramids were built out of big stone blocks. The blocks had to be dug up and cut to size. Then they had to be moved to the right place by sliding them along on wooden rollers. It took lots of men a long time to build a pyramid.

The stone blocks had to be dragged up ramps which got higher and higher.

The Great Pyramid. It took 5,000 men 20 years to build. It is made from over 2,300,000 blocks of stone.

The mummy of the dead pharaoh was put into a small room in the middle of the pyramid. He had lots of things he might need for his next life. There were jewels, food, furniture, pots, and even model dolls to work for him. The entrances were closed up, but the pyramids were often robbed, so the workers made secret rooms to bury the pharaohs in, with traps to catch the thieves.

Everyday life

Egyptian life had a pattern. All the women worked in the home. Most Egyptian men worked at two jobs. When the water in the Nile was low, they worked on the land. Only the most important people and the priests did not farm. When the Nile flooded, the men had other jobs. Some were builders or fishermen. Others were artists or jewelers.

Egyptians had very little furniture.

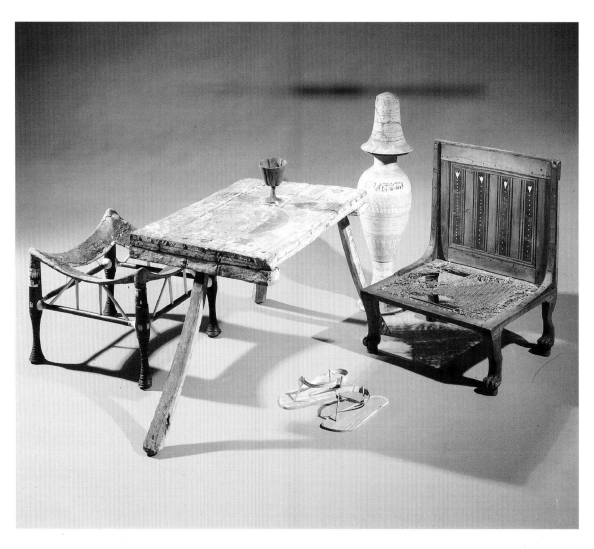

It was very hot in Egypt, so people did not wear many clothes. Men, women, and children wore either thin cloth kilts or robes. Women wore as much makeup and jewelry as they could afford.

To stay cool, people shaved off all their hair. They wore wigs on special occasions.

Egyptian clothes looked a lot like this. The big lumps on the women's heads are scented lumps of fat. They melted in the heat and ran down the women's faces. This kept them cool and made them smell nice.

Houses

The Egyptians built all houses in the same way. The houses of important people had more rooms. They had lovely painted walls inside, but they looked the same on the outside. They used mud bricks for building. The walls were thick, to keep out the heat. Because it did not rain very often, there was no need to have sloping roofs to carry the rain away. The flat roofs were part of the house. People sat on their roofs, or dried washing there. Most people cooked outside, so if they had no yard they did their cooking on the roof too. The houses had rooms under the ground. These rooms were dark and cool. They were very good for storing food and drink.

Inside an Egyptian craftsman's house.

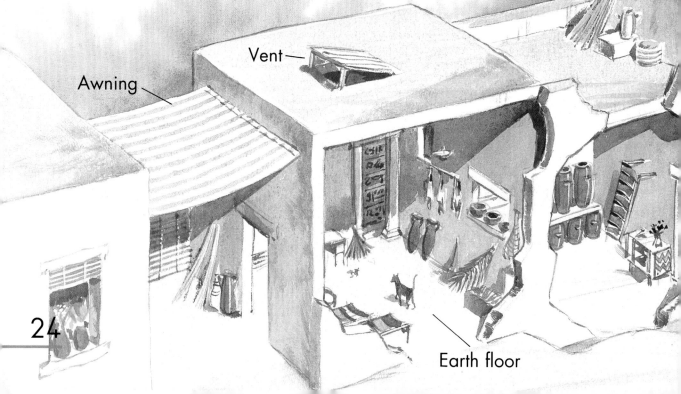

Awning

Vent

Earth floor

*Model of an
Egyptian
house.*

Shrine

Mud bread oven

Cellar

25

Children

Children in Egypt grew up to do the same jobs as their parents. Girls stayed at home with their mothers. They learned how to look after the house, bake bread, and weave flax. Boys went to work with their fathers and helped as much as they could. They only went to school if they were going to work as a scribe.

Very young children stayed at home with their mothers. Many of their games were like games today. They played racing games, tag, and leapfrog. They had balls and wooden toys. Older children played a game like chess, called senet.

Here are some Egyptian children's toys. They are made from wood and reeds.

Medicine

The Egyptians tried to make people well in different ways. They made medicines from plants. They tried to keep clean. Everyone tried to wash their clothes and dishes often.

Making mummies helped the Egyptians learn how the body worked. They saw the lungs, heart, and other organs when they took them out of the body. This helped them to think of better cures.

An Egyptian doctor had many tools.

An ivory charm to keep people safe when they were asleep has pictures of gods and knives to cut wild animals on it.

The magic potion recipe below calls for beetles and a snake's head.

The Egyptians also believed in magic. They thought that evil spirits made people ill. They prayed to a god to make the spirits go away. They drank magic drinks to make them well. They wore magic charms to keep evil spirits away.

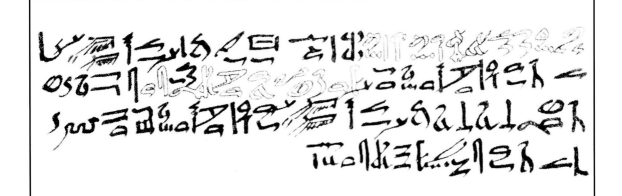

Tutankhamun

Tutankhamun is the most famous of the pharaohs. He was only about eight years old when he became pharaoh. He did not live long enough to fight in a battle and become famous. He did not rule for long enough to be seen as a wise ruler. He is famous just because his people hid his tomb so well that it is the only tomb of a pharaoh that has not been robbed. It was hidden under the tomb of another pharaoh.

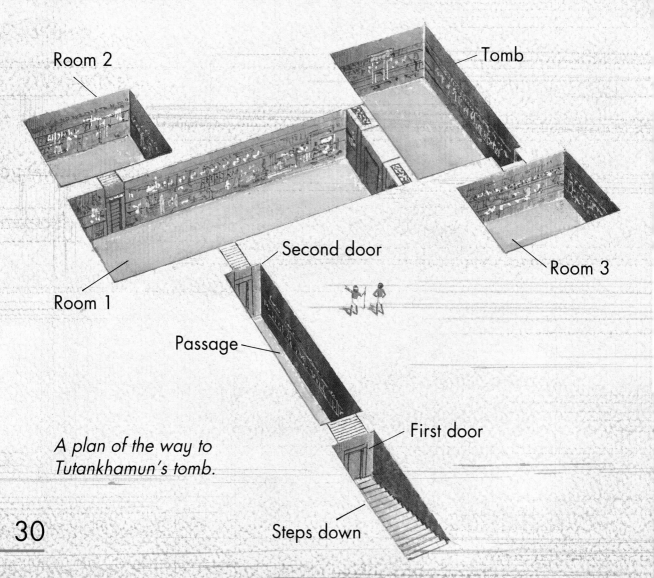

A plan of the way to Tutankhamun's tomb.

Pictured here are just some of the many "wonderful things" that Carter found.

Tutankhamun's tomb was found in 1922. It had several rooms, full of treasure. When diggers made a hole in the wall of the first room, the archaeologist Howard Carter looked in. When asked what he could see, he said, "Wonderful things."

Index

*Please note that Tutankhamun can also be spelled Tutankhamen.